P9-AZV-320

GRAPHIC NONFICTION

ABRAHAM LINCOLN

THE LIFE OF AMERICA'S SIXTEENTH PRESIDENT

by
GARY JEFFREY & KATE PETTY

illustrated by
MIKE LACEY

rosen
central™

The Rosen Publishing Group, Inc., New York

Published in 2005 by The Rosen Publishing Group, Inc.
29 East 21st Street, New York, NY 10010

First edition, 2005

Designed and produced by
David West Books

Editor: Gail Bushnell
Photo Research: Carlotta Cooper

Photo credits:
Pages 6 (both), 7 (both), 44 (top), 45 (bottom) – Mary Evans Picture Library
Page 44 (bottom) – Rex Features Ltd.

Library of Congress Cataloging-in-Publication Data

Jeffrey, Gary.
    Abraham Lincoln : the life of America's sixteenth president / Gary Jeffrey and Kate
Petty.— 1st ed.
    p. cm. — (Graphic nonfiction)
    Includes bibliographical references (p.) and index.
    ISBN 1-4042-0237-4 (lib. bdg.)
    1. Lincoln, Abraham, 1809–1865—Juvenile literature. 2. Presidents—United States—
Biography—Juvenile literature. I. Petty, Kate. II. Title. III. Series.

E457.905.J44 2005
973.7'092—dc22

2004005798

Manufactured in China

CONTENTS

WHO'S WHO

Abraham Lincoln (1809–1865) He became a successful lawyer, congressman, and sixteenth U.S. president (1861–1865). He was also the commander in chief of the Union armed forces during the Civil War.

Jefferson Davis (1808–1889) Former U.S. senator who became president of the Confederate States. He became the commander in chief of their armed forces during the Civil War.

Robert E. Lee (1807–1870) A Virginian who was offered command by both sides, he became the Confederate field commander.

Ulysses S. Grant (1822–1885) Brigadier general in the Union's western field army, lieutenant general of the entire Union armed forces at the end of the Civil War, and then the eighteenth U.S. president.

George B. McClellan (1826–1885) Commander of the Union field army in the East in the first two years of the war. Nicknamed "the little Napoleon."

William T. Sherman (1820–1891) Ohio-born general who became Union commander of the western army at the war's end, taking Atlanta and Savannah.

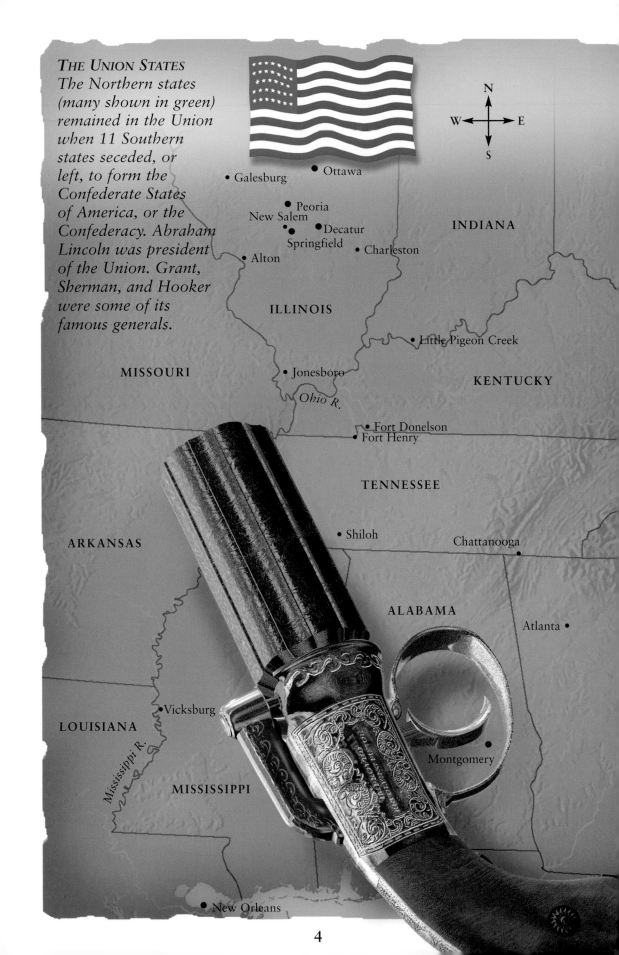

The Union States
The Northern states (many shown in green) remained in the Union when 11 Southern states seceded, or left, to form the Confederate States of America, or the Confederacy. Abraham Lincoln was president of the Union. Grant, Sherman, and Hooker were some of its famous generals.

N
W — E
S

Ottawa

Galesburg

Peoria
New Salem
Decatur
Springfield
Charleston
Alton

INDIANA

ILLINOIS

Little Pigeon Creek

MISSOURI

Jonesboro

KENTUCKY

Ohio R.

Fort Donelson
Fort Henry

TENNESSEE

Shiloh
Chattanooga

ARKANSAS

ALABAMA

Atlanta

Vicksburg

LOUISIANA

Montgomery

Mississippi R.

MISSISSIPPI

New Orleans

4

AMERICA – 1861

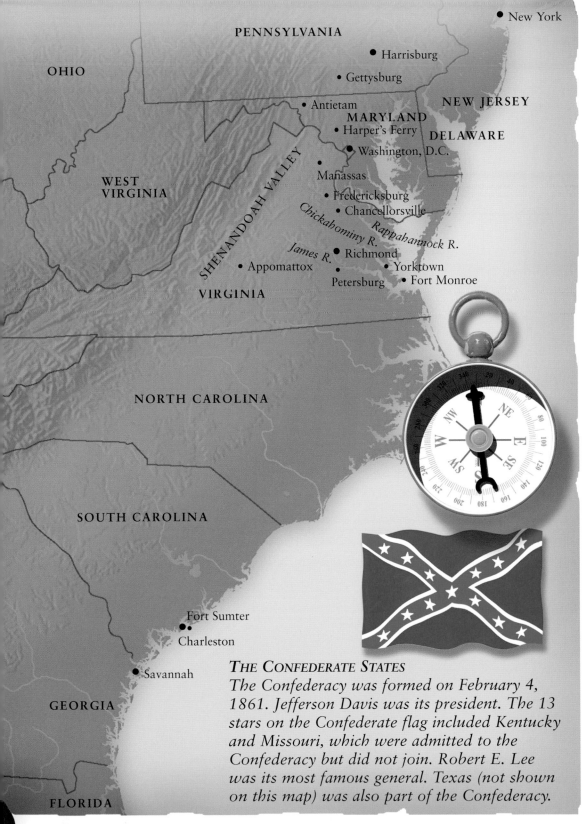

New York

PENNSYLVANIA

OHIO

Harrisburg

Gettysburg

Antietam

NEW JERSEY

MARYLAND

Harper's Ferry

DELAWARE

Washington, D.C.

WEST
VIRGINIA

SHENANDOAH VALLEY

Manassas

Fredericksburg

Chancellorsville

Chickahominy R.

Rappahannock R.

James R.

Richmond

Appomattox

Yorktown

Petersburg

Fort Monroe

VIRGINIA

NORTH CAROLINA

SOUTH CAROLINA

Fort Sumter

Charleston

Savannah

GEORGIA

FLORIDA

THE CONFEDERATE STATES

*The Confederacy was formed on February 4,
1861. Jefferson Davis was its president. The 13
stars on the Confederate flag included Kentucky
and Missouri, which were admitted to the
Confederacy but did not join. Robert E. Lee
was its most famous general. Texas (not shown
on this map) was also part of the Confederacy.*

A DIVIDED NATION

The greatest issue in America when Lincoln came to power in 1860 was slavery. For many years, it had divided the country into two sides: free states in the North and slave states in the South.

SLAVE STATES AND FREE STATES

In a country where all men were supposed to be "free and equal," slavery was still a major problem for Americans in the mid-1800s. Though banned in the "free states" of the North, slavery was still legal in the "slave states" of the South. In these states, plantation owners depended on slave labor to grow tobacco, cotton, and sugar. Abolitionists wanted to ban slavery completely. Lincoln wasn't an abolitionist. He wanted to deal with the problem slowly. He expected Congress to stop slavery from spreading to America's newest territories. His opponents wanted the new territories to be able to choose for themselves.

"Am I not a man and a brother?" Images like this stirred the antislavery movement in the North.

The U.S. Capitol in Washington, D.C., in 1862, before its great iron dome was finished.

THE POLITICAL PARTIES

In the 1850s, the two main political parties were the Whigs and the Democrats. In general, the Whigs were for economic growth and modernization, while the Democrats cared about farming and the land. The Whigs wanted Congress to make decisions on slavery, but the Democrats wanted states to be able to decide for themselves. The slavery issue forced people to change parties or start up new political groups, such as the Liberty Party and the American Party. In 1856, the Whigs became the Republicans.

GOVERNMENT FOR THE PEOPLE

As established in the U.S. Constitution, the federal government of the United States has three branches: an executive, a legislative, and a judicial. The chief executive is the president. The legislature is the two branches of Congress – the Senate and the House of Representatives. The judicial branch is the federal system of courts and judges.

The House of Representatives

FRONTIER LIFE

Settlers like Lincoln's father, Tom, had to clear forests to build homes and plant crops. The wilderness was full of danger. Many people died of disease or hunger if their crops failed.

Settlers often shared their part of the forest with wild animals.

A QUIET AND MELANCHOLY MAN

Abraham was born in a one-room log cabin in the middle of winter. He was named after his grandfather, who had been killed by Native Americans when Tom Lincoln was a boy. Though not the first president to come from a humble background, Abraham grew up to be an unusual man. The tough farmboy did not like killing, and he read everything he could lay his hands on. As an adult, he remained confident in the face of failure. He suffered from depression, which he called his "hypo." Yet despite his depression, Lincoln led America through its darkest hours.

As president, Abraham Lincoln worked to keep the Union together.

ABRAHAM LINCOLN

The Life of America's Sixteenth President

LIFE WAS HARD FOR THE SETTLERS OF LITTLE PIGEON CREEK, INDIANA, IN THE WINTER OF 1816.

AFTER WALKING FOR MILES, TOM LINCOLN AND HIS YOUNG FAMILY ARRIVED AT THE WORST TIME OF YEAR.

TOM HAD TO WAIT UNTIL WINTER HAD PASSED TO BUILD A SOLID LOG CABIN. MEANWHILE, THE FAMILY DID THEIR BEST TO KEEP WARM.

THE FOLLOWING SUMMER, WHILE TOM WAS OFF HUNTING AND HIS WIFE, NANCY, AND THE TWO CHILDREN WERE BUSY PLANTING CORN SEEDS, VISITORS ARRIVED.

ABE, SALLY, MEET MY FAMILY! THEY'VE COME TO LIVE WITH US.

THE FAMILY WAS NANCY'S AUNT AND UNCLE AND HER NEPHEW, DENNIS. THEY SET UP CAMP NEXT DOOR.

THE LINCOLNS WELCOMED THEIR NEW NEIGHBORS. EIGHT-YEAR-OLD ABE GOT ON WELL WITH HIS TEENAGE COUSIN. BUT THEN *TRAGEDY* STRUCK.

NANCY'S AUNT AND UNCLE CAUGHT A MYSTERIOUS ILLNESS CALLED "THE MILK SICK." NANCY NURSED THEM AS WELL AS SHE COULD. BUT BEFORE THE SUMMER'S END THEY WERE DEAD.

THEN NANCY CAUGHT IT.

A WEEK LATER SHE, TOO, WAS DEAD.

TOM MADE HIS WIFE'S COFFIN HIMSELF. YOUNG ABE CARVED THE PEGS FOR THE LID. THEY BURIED NANCY ON A SMALL HILL NEARBY.

WHEN SPRING CAME AGAIN, TOM LINCOLN MADE AN ANNOUNCEMENT TO HIS CHILDREN.

I'M GOING TO KENTUCKY! I'LL BE BACK IN A FEW WEEKS.

"ABE, YOU'RE IN CHARGE OF THE FARM...

DENNIS – YOU'RE IN CHARGE OF ABE...

SALLY – YOU'RE IN CHARGE OF THE HOUSE."

A FEW WEEKS LATER...

CHILDREN! THIS HERE'S YOUR NEW MOTHER. AND YOU'VE GOT TWO NEW SISTERS AND A BROTHER.

THE NEW MRS. LINCOLN EXAMINED ABE AND DENNIS.

TOM! WE NEED TO GET THESE BOYS OUT OF BUCKSKINS AND INTO SOME DENIMS!

SALLY MADE OTHER "IMPROVEMENTS" TO THE LINCOLN HOUSEHOLD. SHE GOT WINDOWS AND FURNITURE FOR THE CABIN AND BOOKS FOR ABE TO STUDY.

WHAT'S THE USE OF BOOKS OUT HERE?

THE BOY SHOULD BE WORKING ...FOR ME!

ABE FELT AS IF HE'D BEEN SPLITTING LOGS, OR RAILS, FOREVER.

THWACK!

THE TERRIBLE, HARD LIFE **SAPPED** THE SPIRIT AND **NUMBED** THE BRAIN.

ABE BEGAN TO DREAM OF ESCAPE...

...BUT HIS FATHER HAD OTHER PLANS.

TOM LINCOLN STARTED TO HIRE OUT HIS TALL, STRONG SON IN EXCHANGE FOR GOODS OR BITS OF SILVER AND TIN THAT PASSED FOR MONEY ON THE FRONTIER. ONE DAY, ABE WAS WORKING ON THE OHIO RIVER, FERRYING PASSENGERS TO CATCH A PASSING STEAMER.

HEY! THIS IS FOR YOU.

IT WAS THE FIRST REAL MONEY ABE HAD EVER BEEN GIVEN. THOUGHTS TUMBLED INTO HIS MIND...

...THOUGHTS OF FREEDOM AND A WORLD BEYOND LITTLE PIGEON CREEK.

WHEN ABRAHAM WAS 22, THE FAMILY MOVED TO A NEW FARM IN MACON COUNTY, ILLINOIS. ALONG WITH HIS STEPBROTHER AND A COUSIN, ABE BUILT AND POLED A FLATBOAT OF GOODS ALL THE WAY DOWN TO NEW ORLEANS.

THEY HAD ARRANGED TO MEET THE OWNER OF THE GOODS IN THE CITY.

ON THE WAY IN, THEY PASSED **SLAVES**...

CRACK!

C'MON, ABE! QUIT **STARING.**

AFTER THAT TRIP, ABRAHAM RETURNED TO AN EMPTY FARM. HIS FAMILY HAD MOVED FARTHER NORTH TO MORE PROMISING LAND.

ABE DECIDED TO STAY PUT. HE HAD A JOB AT THE LOCAL STORE IN NEW SALEM, A NEARBY TOWN.

AT LAST HE WAS FREE OF HIS FATHER.

AND WITH SOME TIME TO READ...

...HE READ...

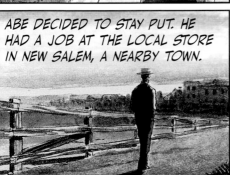

...AND READ!

ABRAHAM'S ODD HABITS AND HEIGHT SOON ATTRACTED THE WRONG KIND OF SMALL-TOWN ATTENTION...

HEY! WHY DON'T YOU STOP READING AND COME OVER HERE?

WHY DON'T YOU **MAKE** ME?

ABE AGREED TO WRESTLE JACK ARMSTRONG.

JACK ARMSTRONG MAY HAVE BEEN AN EXPERIENCED WRESTLER...

HEY!

...BUT HE STILL FOUGHT DIRTY.

THAT HOLD'S ILLEGAL!

ABRAHAM **FLIPPED** HIM.

JACK'S FRIENDS WANTED TO GET EVEN, BUT JACK CALLED THEM OFF. HE AND ABE BECAME FRIENDS.

THE WRESTLING MATCH MADE ABE POPULAR IN NEW SALEM. HE DECIDED TO RUN FOR THE ILLINOIS STATE LEGISLATURE IN 1832.

IF ELECTED, I WILL BE **THANKFUL**. IF BEATEN, I WILL DO AS I HAVE BEEN DOING – WORKING FOR A LIVING!

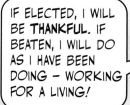

BUT THEN THE STORE FAILED AND ABE WAS OUT OF A JOB.

MEANWHILE, NATIVE AMERICANS LED BY BLACK HAWK HAD CROSSED THE MISSISSIPPI RIVER INTO ILLINOIS IN SEARCH OF LAND.

ABE JOINED THE ARMY TO DRIVE THE INDIANS BACK. HIS MEN CHOSE HIM TO BE THEIR CAPTAIN. HE ALSO MADE SOME POWERFUL FRIENDS. THE EXPERIENCE GAVE HIM CONFIDENCE.

ON HIS RETURN, ABE FELL IN LOVE WITH A GIRL NAMED ANNE RUTLEDGE. SHE WAS THE DAUGHTER OF AN INNKEEPER.

BEFORE THEY COULD GET MARRIED, 23-YEAR-OLD ABRAHAM NEEDED TO EARN SOME MONEY.

ABE BOUGHT OUT THE NEW SALEM STORE, IN PARTNERSHIP WITH WILLIAM BERRY. THEY HAD TO BORROW MONEY FROM THE TOWNSFOLK TO DO IT.

LOOK! LINCOLN'S BUSY GIVING OUT POLITICAL ADVICE WHILE BERRY'S DRINKING AWAY THE PROFITS!

THE STORE SOON FAILED AGAIN.

ABE BECAME POSTMASTER AND THEN DEPUTY COUNTY SURVEYOR, BEFORE BEING ELECTED TO THE STATE LEGISLATURE AS A WHIG IN 1834. HE WAS HELPED BY A FRIEND FROM THE BLACK HAWK CAMPAIGN, COLONEL JOHN T. STUART...

ABRAHAM, IF YOU'RE REALLY **SERIOUS** ABOUT POLITICS YOU NEED TO STUDY THE LAW.

ABE DECIDED TO BECOME A LAWYER, MAKE HIS FORTUNE, AND THEN PROPOSE TO ANNE.

BUT SADLY, ANNE RUTLEDGE *DIED* OF FEVER IN 1835.

A **CHANGE** CAME OVER ABRAHAM. SOME DESCRIBED IT AS A DEEP **MELANCHOLY**. LINCOLN CALLED IT HIS "HYPO" AND IT WOULD NOW BE A CONSTANT PROBLEM.

BY THE SPRING OF 1837, LINCOLN WAS LEADER OF THE LOCAL WHIG PARTY. HE MOVED TO THE NEW STATE CAPITAL OF SPRINGFIELD AND JOINED THE LAW PRACTICE OF JOHN STUART, WHO WAS NOW A MEMBER OF CONGRESS.

IN 1842, ABE MARRIED MARY TODD, A SPIRITED WIDOW FROM A GOOD KENTUCKY FAMILY.

THEY BOUGHT A HOUSE...

...AND HAD TWO SONS, ROBERT AND EDDIE.

IN 1844, ABE SET UP HIS OWN LAW PRACTICE IN THE CENTER OF SPRINGFIELD. BILLY HERNDON WAS HIS ASSISTANT.

ABE FINALLY WAS ELECTED TO THE HOUSE OF REPRESENTATIVES. IN 1847, HE WENT TO WASHINGTON WITH MARY AND THEIR SONS.

LIKE MOST WHIGS, LINCOLN WAS AGAINST THE SPREAD OF SLAVERY INTO THE NEW TERRITORIES. HIS REASONS WERE PRACTICAL.

I USED TO BE A "SLAVE," BUT I MADE MYSELF **FREE,** AND I AM NOW **SO** FREE THAT THEY LET ME **PRACTICE LAW.**

LINCOLN FELT THAT POOR WHITE MEN COULD NOT COMPETE FOR WORK AGAINST CHEAP SLAVE LABOR. IT MADE IT HARDER FOR THEM TO EARN A LIVING.

BUT STEPHEN DOUGLAS, LINCOLN'S DEMOCRAT RIVAL, THOUGHT SLAVERY SHOULD BE ALLOWED TO SPREAD.

THEN LINCOLN ATTACKED AMERICA'S WAR AGAINST MEXICO. HE WAS SHOUTED DOWN FOR BEING UNPATRIOTIC. IN MARCH 1849, HIS FIRST TERM IN CONGRESS CAME TO AN END.

ABE RETURNED TO SPRINGFIELD.

BILLY, I'M POLITICALLY **DEAD.** FROM NOW ON I WANT TO DEVOTE MYSELF **ENTIRELY** TO THIS PRACTICE.

IN 1850, THE LINCOLNS' YOUNGER SON, EDDIE, WHO WAS ALMOST FOUR, DIED FROM TUBERCULOSIS. MARY WAS BESIDE HERSELF WITH GRIEF. LATER SHE WOULD HAVE TWO MORE BOYS, WILLIE AND TAD.

OVER THE NEXT FEW YEARS, THE LAW PRACTICE FLOURISHED.

LINCOLN WON MANY CASES. HE BECAME FAMOUS FOR THE "SLEDGEHAMMER LOGIC" OF HIS ARGUMENTS.

BUT HE **STILL** FOUND TIME TO BE A DEVOTED FATHER TO HIS THREE SONS.

MEANWHILE, TROUBLE WAS BREWING AS STEPHEN DOUGLAS ADDRESSED THE SENATE...

"I PROPOSE THAT THE CITIZENS OF THE NEWLY CREATED STATES OF KANSAS AND NEBRASKA SHALL DECIDE FOR **THEMSELVES** WHETHER OR NOT TO ADMIT **SLAVERY** TO THEIR TERRITORIES."

UNTIL THIS TIME, **CONGRESS** HAD ALWAYS DECIDED WHETHER NEW STATES SHOULD BE **SLAVE** OR **FREE**. THE DECISION PROCESS TOOK A LONG TIME. WITH HIS BILL, DOUGLAS HOPED TO SETTLE THE ISSUE ONCE AND FOR ALL.

IN MAY 1854, THE BILL WAS PASSED. LINCOLN WAS OUTRAGED...

SENATOR DOUGLAS HAS **SOLD US OUT!**

"THE WEST SHOULD BE A HOME FOR FREE WHITE PEOPLE. **SLAVE STATES** ARE THE PLACES THE POOR TRY TO **LEAVE**, NOT **GO!**"

LATER THAT YEAR, IN PEORIA, ILLINOIS, LINCOLN SPOKE OUT AGAINST DOUGLAS'S KANSAS-NEBRASKA ACT.

ONCE SLAVERY IS IN THE FIRST FEW STATES IT WILL BE VERY HARD TO GET IT **OUT OF THE MANY...**

"...MY FAITH TEACHES ME THAT 'ALL **MEN** ARE CREATED **EQUAL.'** THERE CAN BE NO MORAL RIGHT IN ONE **MAN'S** MAKING A SLAVE OF ANOTHER."

THE SPEECH WON LINCOLN THE SEAT IN ILLINOIS BUT HE TURNED IT DOWN.

I INTEND TO FIGHT THIS ON A BIGGER STAGE!

HE NARROWLY MISSED GETTING INTO THE SENATE THIS TIME.

ABE WENT TO A BIG MEETING ORGANIZED BY SEVERAL DIFFERENT GROUPS IN ILLINOIS WHO WERE ALL OPPOSED TO THE DOUGLAS BILL. THEY CALLED THEMSELVES **REPUBLICANS**.

LINCOLN JOINED THEM. HE GAVE SUCH A ROUSING SPEECH THAT LATER IN THE YEAR HE WAS ASKED TO BE THE REPUBLICAN CANDIDATE FOR VICE PRESIDENT.

AGAIN LINCOLN NARROWLY LOST. THE DEMOCRAT CANDIDATE, **JAMES BUCHANAN**, WON. VOTERS HOPED BUCHANAN WOULD BE ABLE TO CALM DOWN THE SLAVERY ISSUE.

IT WAS NOT TO BE. IN 1857, DRED SCOTT, A SLAVE WHOSE MASTER HAD DIED, CLAIMED THAT LIVING IN ILLINOIS FOR EIGHT YEARS HAD MADE HIM LEGALLY FREE.

YOU ARE NOT A U.S. CITIZEN, SO YOU **CANNOT** SUE THE GOVERNMENT!

BUT THE COURTS HAD OTHER IDEAS.

THIS TIME **EVERYONE** WAS OUTRAGED. THEN BUCHANAN DECIDED TO ADMIT KANSAS AS A SLAVE STATE **WHATEVER** THE OUTCOME OF A POPULAR VOTE. IT PROVED TOO MUCH FOR DOUGLAS. HE PUBLICLY OPPOSED HIS PRESIDENT AND SOME REPUBLICANS BEGAN TO PRAISE HIM FOR IT.

DOUGLAS IS A **DODGER**, A **WRIGGLER**. A **TOOL OF THE SOUTH** ONCE AND NOW A **SNAPPER** AT IT!

LINCOLN STUDIED THE DRED SCOTT CASE SO HE COULD ATTACK BOTH SIDES OF THE DIVIDED DEMOCRATS ON **SLAVERY**.

WHEN THE REPUBLICANS OF ILLINOIS NEXT ASSEMBLED, THEY MADE LINCOLN THEIR "FIRST AND ONLY CHOICE" FOR THE SENATE. IN THE EVENING HE GAVE A SPEECH...

"A HOUSE **DIVIDED AGAINST ITSELF** CANNOT STAND...

...THIS GOVERNMENT CANNOT ENDURE, PERMANENTLY **HALF-SLAVE** AND **HALF-FREE**. I DO NOT EXPECT THE **UNION** TO BE DISSOLVED. I DO NOT EXPECT THIS HOUSE TO **FALL**...IT WILL BECOME **ALL ONE THING** OR **ALL THE OTHER**."

LINCOLN'S SPEECH CAUSED A STORM...

HE WENT TOO FAR! THAT SPEECH WILL BE THE DOWNFALL OF LINCOLN **AND** OF THE REPUBLICAN PARTY!

THEY SAY YOU'RE THREATENING **CIVIL WAR** OVER SLAVERY!

YOU NEED TO PUT YOUR CASE TO **THE PEOPLE.**

LINCOLN AGREED.

I WILL DEBATE WITH DOUGLAS. WE'LL BOTH PUT OUR CASES TO AN AUDIENCE.

A CHALLENGE WAS SENT TO DOUGLAS.

I ACCEPT!

THEY AGREED TO MEET IN SEVEN OF THE CONGRESSIONAL DISTRICTS IN ILLINOIS. THEY BEGAN AT OTTAWA, WHERE DOUGLAS SPOKE FIRST...

...THE **FOUNDING FATHERS** CREATED THE CONSTITUTION HALF-SLAVE AND HALF-FREE...LINCOLN'S DOCTRINES WILL COVER YOUR PRAIRIES WITH **BLACK SETTLEMENTS**...TURN THIS BEAUTIFUL STATE INTO A FREE **NEGRO COLONY!**

THE CROWD **MURMURED**, BUT NOW IT WAS **LINCOLN'S** TURN...

"WE WILL NOT SETTLE THE QUESTION UNTIL THE **OPPONENTS** OF SLAVERY **PREVENT** THE FURTHER **SPREAD** OF IT..."

...IN THE RIGHT TO EAT THE **BREAD OF HIS LABOR** WITHOUT THE LEAVE OF ANYONE ELSE, THE SLAVE IS MY **EQUAL,** AND THE EQUAL OF **JUDGE DOUGLAS,** AND THE EQUAL OF **EVERY LIVING MAN!**

THE CROWD CHEERED. HE HAD STARTED WELL.

16

DOUGLAS SEEMED TO HAVE THE UPPER HAND IN THE NEXT FOUR DEBATES. THE FINAL MEETING WAS IN ALTON, ON THE MISSISSIPPI. LINCOLN'S WIFE AND SON WERE THERE TO SUPPORT HIM, BUT ANTI-REPUBLICAN FEELING WAS RUNNING HIGH AMONG THE CROWD AS HE STOOD UP TO MAKE HIS FINAL SPEECH...

"WHETHER IT COMES FROM THE **MOUTH OF A KING** WHO SEEKS TO BESTRIDE THE PEOPLE OF HIS OWN NATION AND LIVE BY THE FRUIT OF THEIR LABOR...

...OR FROM ONE RACE OF MEN AS AN **APOLOGY** FOR ENSLAVING ANOTHER RACE, IT IS THE SAME **TYRANNICAL PRINCIPLE!**"

THE CROWD ROARED!

LINCOLN HOPED HIS PERFORMANCE WOULD INCREASE HIS CHANCES OF BEATING DOUGLAS TO BECOME THE ILLINOIS SENATOR IN 1859. BUT YET AGAIN, HE NARROWLY LOST.

THE **HYPO** DESCENDED UPON HIM.

I FEEL LIKE THE BOY WHO STUBBED HIS TOE — TOO **BIG** TO CRY AND TOO **BADLY HURT** TO LAUGH...

BUT, IN FACT, HIS FAME AS A POLITICIAN WAS BEGINNING TO SPREAD.

YOU'RE THE TALK OF THE TOWN IN THE EAST, THEY SAY YOU SHOULD RUN FOR **PRESIDENT.**

I DO NOT THINK MYSELF FIT FOR THE PRESIDENCY...

...I REALLY THINK IT BEST FOR OUR CAUSE THAT WE DON'T TRY TOO HARD FOR IT.

BUT THE WHEELS OF HISTORY WERE ALREADY TURNING. NEWS CAME OF A FAILED ATTEMPT BY ABOLITIONIST JOHN BROWN TO START A SLAVE REBELLION IN VIRGINIA. SLAVERY WAS A HOTTER TOPIC THAN EVER.

EARLY IN 1860, LINCOLN'S SUPPORTERS STARTED TO PLAN HIS NOMINATION AS THE ILLINOIS REPUBLICAN CANDIDATE FOR THE **PRESIDENCY**.

MEANWHILE, LINCOLN ACCEPTED AN INVITATION TO SPEAK TO THE REPUBLICANS IN NEW YORK.

...THOMAS JEFFERSON SAID, IT IS POSSIBLE FOR US TO FREE THE SLAVES AND DEPORT THEM GRADUALLY, SO THE CHANGE WILL TAKE PLACE SLOWLY AND PEACEFULLY. THEN THEIR PLACES CAN BE FILLED BY **FREE WHITE LABORERS**...

"...IF SLAVERY IS **RIGHT**, ALL WORDS, ACTS, LAWS, AND CONSTITUTIONS AGAINST IT, ARE THEMSELVES **WRONG**, AND SHOULD BE **SILENCED, AND SWEPT AWAY.**"

AT THE OFFICES OF THE NEW YORK TRIBUNE THE FOLLOWING DAY...

THE SPEECH WAS **SUPERB!** THEY SAID LINCOLN WAS THE GREATEST MAN SINCE **SAINT PAUL!**

IN THE EDITOR'S OFFICE...

YOU KNOW, THIS MAN LINCOLN — **HE MIGHT JUST DO IT.**

LINCOLN FACED TOUGH COMPETITION FROM WILLIAM H. SEWARD. SEWARD WAS ALREADY THE FAVORITE TO BE THE REPUBLICAN CANDIDATE FOR PRESIDENT.

MAY 1860 – ILLINOIS REPUBLICAN CONVENTION, DECATUR.

HEY! LOOK AT THAT!

ABRAHAM LINCOLN THE RAIL SPLITTER CANDIDATE FOR PRESIDENT IN 1860

THE CROWD LOVED THE BANNER CARRIED BY ABE'S COUSIN.

LINCOLN DIDN'T...

BUT...

YOU'VE BEEN NOMINATED!

NOW I'LL BE FOREVER KNOWN AS **HONEST ABE THE RAIL SPLITTER!**

LINCOLN'S TEAM WENT TO CHICAGO TO DRUM UP REPUBLICAN SUPPORT ON A NATIONAL LEVEL.

A FEW WEEKS LATER, LINCOLN WAITED AT HIS OFFICE TO HEAR THE RESULT OF THE VOTE IN CHICAGO...

I ARISE, MR. CHAIRMAN, TO ANNOUNCE THE CHANGE OF **FOUR** VOTES ...TO ABRAHAM LINCOLN!

REPORTERS SPREAD THE NEWS...

AT THE RESULT, THE CROWD **ROARED** LIKE ALL THE HOGS EVER SLAUGHTERED IN CINCINNATI **MAKING THEIR DEATH SQUEALS TOGETHER!**

LINCOLN HAD BEATEN SEWARD! HE WOULD RUN FOR PRESIDENT!

OVER THE NEXT FEW DAYS, HIS HOUSE WAS SURROUNDED BY WELL-WISHERS.

I'D INVITE YOU ALL IN, IF ONLY THE PLACE WERE **BIGGER!**

DON'T WORRY – WE'LL GET YOU A LARGER PLACE WHEN YOU TAKE OFFICE!

THE RACE FOR THE PRESIDENCY WAS ON.

MEANWHILE, IN THE DEMOCRATS' CAMP, DELEGATES FROM THE SOUTHERN STATES WALKED OUT IN PROTEST AT STEPHEN DOUGLAS'S NOMINATION. THEY NOMINATED VICE PRESIDENT JOHN BRECKINRIDGE INSTEAD.

BACK AT LINCOLN'S CAMPAIGN HEADQUARTERS...

THIS SPLIT IN THE DEMOCRATS REALLY GIVES US A CHANCE!

YES, BUT HAVE YOU **SEEN** THESE SOUTHERN PAPERS?

I'M SHOWN AS SOME KIND OF **TYRANT**.

THEY SAY THAT I PLAN TO URGE THE SLAVES TO RISE UP! WHAT CAN I SAY TO REASSURE THEM?

SOUTHERNERS BLAMED REPUBLICANS FOR JOHN BROWN'S FAILED UPRISING.

NOVEMBER 6, 1860. ELECTION DAY. CROWDS GATHERED IN SPRINGFIELD TOWN SQUARE TO HEAR THE FINAL RESULTS. ABRAHAM WAS GOING TO BE **PRESIDENT!**

HE'S GOT NEW YORK!

HOORRRAY!

WELL, BOYS, YOUR TROUBLES ARE OVER NOW. MINE HAVE JUST BEGUN!

BRECKINRIDGE HAD CARRIED THE SOUTH BUT LINCOLN HAD WON MOST OF THE NORTH, GIVING HIM THE MAJORITY.

TROUBLE WAS BREWING ALREADY. THE GOVERNOR OF SOUTH CAROLINA CALLED AN EMERGENCY SESSION OF HIS STATE LEGISLATURE. HE WANTED SOUTH CAROLINA TO LEAVE THE UNION AND START A SOUTHERN CONFEDERACY.

BY THE BEGINNING OF FEBRUARY 1861, MISSISSIPPI, FLORIDA, ALABAMA, GEORGIA, LOUISIANA, AND TEXAS HAD JOINED SOUTH CAROLINA. THE **CONFEDERACY** WAS BORN.

AT THE SAME TIME A CAUTIOUS ABRAHAM LEFT FOR WASHINGTON.

BILLY, LEAVE THE SIGN HANGING UP...

...IF I LIVE, I'M COMING BACK SOMETIME, AND THEN WE'LL GO RIGHT ON PRACTICING LAW AS IF NOTHING HAD EVER HAPPENED.

WHILE PRESIDENT-ELECT LINCOLN WAS ON HIS WAY TO WASHINGTON, IN MONTGOMERY, ALABAMA, **ANOTHER PRESIDENT** WAS BEING SWORN IN. **PRESIDENT JEFFERSON DAVIS** SPOKE TO HIS SUPPORTERS...

OBSTACLES MAY STAND IN OUR WAY BUT THEY CANNOT PREVENT OUR PROGRESS. OUR MOVEMENT IS A FAIR ONE AND OUR SUPPORTERS ARE GOOD PEOPLE.

IN THE SOUTH, **UNION** INSTITUTIONS AND BUILDINGS WERE BEING TURNED OVER TO THE **CONFEDERATES**. THE UNION FORTS WERE **EVACUATED** UNTIL JUST ONE SMALL STRONGHOLD REMAINED IN CHARLESTON BAY, SOUTH CAROLINA...

...FORT SUMTER.

THE SOUTH CAROLINA MILITIA **DEMANDED** ITS SURRENDER.

WE WILL **NEVER** SURRENDER!

IT WAS TO BE PRESIDENT BUCHANAN'S **LAST ACT**.

MARCH 4, 1861, INAUGURATION DAY.

WITH ARMED GUARDS AT EVERY WINDOW OF THE CAPITOL, THE NEW PRESIDENT STOOD UP TO SPEAK.

IN **YOUR** HANDS, MY DISSATISFIED FELLOW-COUNTRYMEN, AND NOT IN **MINE**, IS THE MOMENTOUS ISSUE OF **CIVIL WAR**. THE GOVERNMENT WILL NOT ASSAIL YOU. YOU CAN HAVE NO CONFLICT WITHOUT BEING YOURSELVES THE **AGGRESSORS**.

I HAVE NO PURPOSE, DIRECTLY OR INDIRECTLY, TO **INTERFERE** WITH THE INSTITUTION OF SLAVERY IN **THE STATES WHERE IT EXISTS**. I BELIEVE I HAVE NO LAWFUL RIGHT TO DO SO, AND I HAVE NO INCLINATION TO DO SO.

THE NEW PRESIDENT DID NOT WANT TO START A CIVIL WAR, SO HE MADE NEW APPOINTMENTS INSTEAD.

THE PRESIDENT WILL SEE YOU NOW, MR. SMITH.

I FEEL LIKE A MAN LETTING OUT THE LODGINGS AT **ONE** END OF HIS HOUSE WHILE THE **OTHER** END IS ON **FIRE.**

SOON, IN A MEETING WITH HIS ADVISERS...

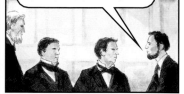

FORT SUMTER ONLY HAS SUPPLIES FOR ANOTHER FOUR WEEKS. SOMETHING HAS TO BE DONE.

IT WILL TAKE A **THIRD** OF THE ARMY TO RELIEVE SUMTER!

WE SHOULD **GET OUR MEN OUT OF THE FORT NOW.** LET THE SOUTH **HAVE IT.**

GENTLEMEN...

WE WILL SEND OUR NAVY **WITH SUPPLIES.** IF THE REBELS BEGIN **FIRING,** THE CHOICE WILL BE ON **THEIR** HEADS, NOT **OURS.**

ON APRIL 12, 1861, CONFEDERATE PRESIDENT DAVIS ORDERED HIS SOLDIERS TO OPEN FIRE ON FORT SUMTER. THE FORT **SURRENDERED 34** HOURS LATER.

THE WAR WAS ON. LINCOLN CALLED UP A 75,000-MAN MILITIA ON A THREE-MONTH SERVICE TO **PUT DOWN THE REBELLION.**

IN THE SOUTH, **FOUR** MORE STATES LEFT THE UNION – NORTH CAROLINA, ARKANSAS, TENNESSEE, AND VIRGINIA. MARYLAND, MISSOURI, AND KENTUCKY WERE UNDECIDED.

IN THE WHITE HOUSE, LINCOLN'S ASSISTANT *JOHN NICOLAY* TURNED HIS TELESCOPE ACROSS THE RIVER TOWARD VIRGINIA.

THERE'S A **CONFEDERATE FLAG** FLYING IN ALEXANDRIA! WE'RE WIDE OPEN TO **ATTACK!**

WORSE STILL, THE CONFEDERATES HAD MOVED THEIR CAPITAL FROM MONTGOMERY TO RICHMOND, JUST 120 MILES FROM WASHINGTON. THOUSANDS OF UNION SOLDIERS WERE RUSHED IN TO PROTECT WASHINGTON FROM A POSSIBLE INVASION.

ONE DAY AS HE INSPECTED TROOPS AT THE WHITE HOUSE, LINCOLN SPOTTED A FAMILIAR FACE...

WHY, ELMER!

ELMER ELLSWORTH, A FAMILY FRIEND FROM SPRINGFIELD, HAD BEEN MADE A CAPTAIN OF HIS ZOUAVE UNIT.

THE BOYS WILL BE PLEASED TO SEE YOU!

NOT LONG AFTER, ELMER LED HIS COMPANY TO ALEXANDRIA TO REMOVE THE CONFEDERATE FLAG THAT WAS FLYING ON MARSHAL'S TAVERN.

AS HE CAME DOWNSTAIRS HE MET THE INNKEEPER...

AAAAGH!

BLAM!

THE ZOUAVES FOUGHT BACK BUT ELMER WAS DEAD.

ARRRGH!

CRACK!

ABE AND MARY WERE VERY SAD TO LOSE THEIR FRIEND.

AS THE WEEKS PASSED, ABE WAS PRESSURED TO USE THE MILITIA AGAINST THE CONFEDERATES BEFORE THEIR 90-DAYS' SERVICE ENDED.

THE PUBLIC ARE SCREAMING FOR ACTION. WE MUST AVENGE SUMTER!

LINCOLN SENT FOR THE NEW ARMY'S COMMANDER, IRVIN MCDOWELL.

SIR, I HAVE TO WARN YOU, THE ARMY IS NOT YET READY FOR A MAJOR BATTLE!

YOU ARE GREEN, IT'S TRUE, BUT THE REBELS ARE GREEN ALSO; YOU ARE ALL GREEN ALIKE.

LINCOLN ORDERED THE MILITIA TO ADVANCE ON RICHMOND. HE HOPED A DECISIVE STRIKE WOULD END THE WAR QUICKLY.

LINCOLN'S **UNION ARMY** FACED 24,000 CONFEDERATE SOLDIERS COMMANDED BY **GENERAL PIERRE BEAUREGARD** AT MANASSAS IN NORTHERN VIRGINIA. TO THE WEST WAS ANOTHER CONFEDERATE ARMY, COMMANDED BY **GENERAL THOMAS J. JACKSON**. THE UNION COMMAND HAD SENT A FORCE UNDER **GENERAL PATTERSON** TO STOP JACKSON'S MEN FROM JOINING THE BATTLE.

UNION SPIRITS WERE HIGH AS THE MEN ARRIVED AND BEGAN CROSSING THE **BULL RUN STREAM.** MEANWHILE, **JACKSON** HAD MANAGED TO GIVE **PATTERSON** THE SLIP.

HE WAS ON HIS WAY.

AT 6:30 A.M. ON JULY 21, 1861, THE UNION AND CONFEDERATE ARMIES MET IN BATTLE. AT FIRST, THE UNION'S GREATER NUMBERS WERE TOO MUCH FOR THE CONFEDERATES.

BUT THEN, WHEN JACKSON WAS GIVEN THE NEWS...

GENERAL JACKSON, THEY'RE BEATING US BACK!

SIR, WE WILL GIVE THEM **THE BAYONET!**

"STONEWALL" JACKSON HAD ARRIVED.

FORM! FORM! THERE STANDS JACKSON LIKE A STONE WALL! RALLY BEHIND THE VIRGINIANS!

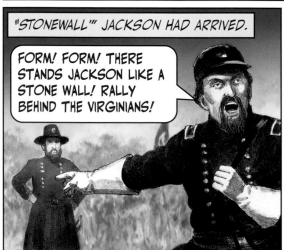

LATER ON, A FORCE OF **VIRGINIANS**, WEARING SIMILAR UNIFORMS TO THE UNION SOLDIERS, MARCHED UP TO A **UNION GUN LINE...**

...AND UNLEASHED THEIR FURY.

THE CONFEDERATES NOW HAD THE UPPER HAND. THE UNION RETREAT TURNED INTO A **BLOODBATH**.

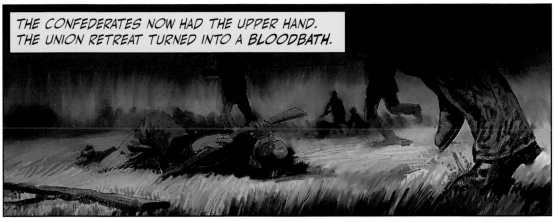

BY LATE AFTERNOON, WOUNDED AND EXHAUSTED TROOPS WERE POURING ONTO THE STREETS OF **WASHINGTON**.

LINCOLN HEARD THE NEWS...

BULL RUN SHOWED THAT THIS CONFLICT WAS GOING TO BE NEITHER **SHORT** NOR **EASY**. LINCOLN'S ADVISERS SUGGESTED A NEW COMMANDER FOR THE MILITIA, **GEORGE B. MCCLELLAN**. HE WAS HIGHLY SKILLED AND THE MEN LOVED HIM. HE WAS GIVEN **500,000** NEW LONG-TERM VOLUNTEERS TO TURN INTO AN ARMY.

THE "LITTLE NAPOLEON" MADE HIS POWER FELT EVERYWHERE. HE DRILLED AND EQUIPPED THE MOST MAGNIFICENT FIGHTING FORCE AMERICA **HAD EVER SEEN**.

BUT WHEN ASKED TO MAKE A PLAN OF ATTACK, HE **STALLED**.

WHEN AT LAST MCCLELLAN **DID COME** UP WITH A PLAN, LINCOLN WAS **UNEASY**.

IT LEAVES WASHINGTON **EXPOSED**...

BUT HE AGREED WITH HIS COMMANDERS.

I DON'T CARE, GENTLEMEN, **WHAT** PLAN YOU HAVE. ALL I ASK IS FOR YOU TO **JUST PITCH IN!**

MEANWHILE, IN THE WEST, **BRIGADIER GENERAL ULYSSES S. GRANT** HAD BECOME A NORTHERN HERO. HIS UNION FORCES HAD WON BATTLES AT FORT HENRY AND FORT DONELSON.

EARLY IN 1862, MCCLELLAN'S ARMY OF 130,000 FINALLY GOT READY FOR ACTION. MCCLELLAN DECIDED TO LAND HIS MEN ON THE PENINSULA AT FORT MONROE, VIRGINIA, AND MARCH WEST. THEN THEY WOULD TAKE YORKTOWN AND MAKE RICHMOND GIVE UP BY **POUNDING** IT WITH HEAVY GUNS.

MCCLELLAN SPOKE TO HIS TROOPS...

I WILL BRING YOU FACE-TO-FACE WITH THE REBELS AND IT SHALL BE MY CARE TO GAIN **SUCCESS** WITH THE **LEAST POSSIBLE LOSS.**

AT HOME, LINCOLN WAS CRUSHED BY THE DEATH OF HIS FAVORITE SON, 12-YEAR-OLD WILLIE.

ON APRIL 5, WHEN HIS ARMY REACHED YORKTOWN, MCCLELLAN WIRED LINCOLN.

HE THINKS HE'S FACING **THE WHOLE REBEL ARMY.** HE WANTS TO **BESIEGE** YORKTOWN RATHER THAN RISK AN **ADVANCE.**

LINCOLN SENT A REPLY...

I think you had better break the enemy's line **at once**...I have never written to you in **greater kindness**, nor with **fuller purpose** to sustain you...**but you must act!**

MCCLELLAN READ LINCOLN'S TELEGRAPH.

I AM TEMPTED TO REPLY THAT HE HAD BETTER **COME** DO IT HIMSELF.

MEANWHILE, GRANT WAS RESTING HIS ARMY OUT WEST IN SHILOH, WESTERN TENNESSEE, WITH HIS SECOND-IN-COMMAND, WILLIAM SHERMAN.

GRANT, THIS IS QUITE THE **BEST** CAMP WE'VE EVER HAD. I HAVE SCARCELY THE FAINTEST IDEA OF AN ATTACK BEING MADE ON US HERE.

BUT THAT NIGHT, LESS THAN A MILE AWAY, CONFEDERATE **GENERAL ALBERT S. JOHNSTON** WAS SPEAKING WITH HIS COMMANDERS ON HOW BEST TO GIVE GRANT AND SHERMAN A SURPRISE IN THE MORNING.

AT 9:30 A.M. THEY **ATTACKED**, CHASING THE UNION SOLDIERS FROM THEIR CAMP. JOHNSTON AND GENERAL BEAUREGARD WATCHED THE BATTLE FROM A HILLTOP.

WE ARE SWEEPING THE FIELD! I THINK WE SHALL **PRESS** THEM TO THE **RIVER!**

GRANT ARRIVED FROM HIS HEADQUARTERS UPRIVER TO FIND THE LANDING LITTERED WITH **WOUNDED** UNION MEN.

THE SITUATION WAS DESPERATE.

GENERAL GRANT, THERE'S **ONE THIN LINE** IN OUR CENTER THAT'S STILL HOLDING...

EARLY IN THE BATTLE, UNION GENERAL PRENTISS STAYED BACK WITH HIS SOLDIERS ON A ROAD IN THE WOODS.

TO YOUR BATTERIES! HERE COME THE REBELS!

THE CONFEDERATES ATTACKED A DOZEN TIMES. EACH TIME THEY WERE DRIVEN BACK. THE FIRE WAS SO THICK, THE AREA BECAME KNOWN AS THE **HORNETS' NEST**.

DURING THE FIGHT, GRANT CAME UP TO SEE **PRENTISS**.

YOU **MUST** HOLD ON – AT ALL COSTS.

BUT BY LATE AFTERNOON, THE UNION MEN COULD NOT HOLD ON ANY LONGER. THE CONFEDERATES PUT 62 CANNONS ON THE THICKET AND **OPENED FIRE**. THE GENERAL HAD TO **SURRENDER**, BUT HIS STAND HAD SAVED THE DAY.

WE'LL BEAT THEM TOMORROW.

IN THE EVENING, THE FIGHTING STOPPED. GENERAL SHERMAN WENT TO FIND GRANT.

WE HAD A TERRIBLE DAY TODAY, DIDN'T WE?

THIRTEEN HUNDRED DEAD AND WOUNDED! GRANT'S A BUTCHER!

HE SHOULD BE REMOVED IMMEDIATELY!

SECRETARY STANTON, I CAN'T SPARE THIS MAN - HE FIGHTS.

BUT GRANT WAS TEMPORARILY REMOVED FROM THE ROLE OF COMMANDER.

MEANWHILE, ON THE *MISSISSIPPI*, A GREAT FIREFIGHT WAS TAKING PLACE...

...AS DAVID *FARRAGUT* PUSHED 22 SHIPS NORTHWARD PAST CONFEDERATE RIVER FORTS UNDER A *HAIL OF FIRE* TO TAKE NEW ORLEANS, LOUISIANA.

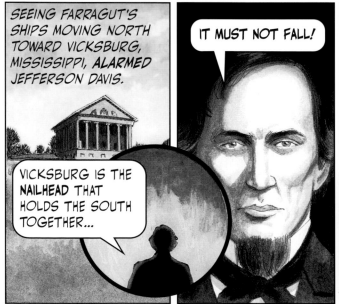

SEEING FARRAGUT'S SHIPS MOVING NORTH TOWARD VICKSBURG, MISSISSIPPI, *ALARMED* JEFFERSON DAVIS.

VICKSBURG IS THE *NAILHEAD* THAT HOLDS THE SOUTH TOGETHER...

IT MUST NOT FALL!

BUT WHEN FARRAGUT REACHED VICKSBURG...

MY SHIPS CANNOT CRAWL UP HILLS *300 FEET HIGH*...

...WE NEED AN *ARMY*.

BACK IN VIRGINIA, MCCLELLAN'S MEN WERE GETTING CLOSE TO RICHMOND, THE CONFEDERATE CAPITAL. THEY HAD NEARBY YORKTOWN UNDER SIEGE UNTIL THE CONFEDERATES ABANDONED IT. MCCLELLAN HALTED HIS ADVANCE AND TELEGRAPHED WASHINGTON.

HE WANTS ANOTHER **40,000** MEN SENT WITH MCDOWELL BEFORE HE'LL **ATTACK.**

THIS TIME STANTON **EXPLODED...**

IF HE HAD A **MILLION** MEN HE WOULD SWEAR THE ENEMY HAD **TWO MILLION** AND THEN WOULD SIT IN THE MUD AND YELL FOR **THREE!**

AFTER A VICTORY NEAR THE CHICKAHOMINY RIVER, MCCLELLAN'S TROOPS WAITED AT THE RIVER'S EDGE FOR A MONTH. MANY OF THEM CAUGHT DISEASES. IN A BATTLE AT SEVEN PINES, THE CONFEDERATE COMMANDER, **JOSEPH E. JOHNSTON,** WAS WOUNDED.

JOHNSTON'S REPLACEMENT, THE MILITARY ADVISER **ROBERT E. LEE,** WAS SUMMONED TO SEE DAVIS...

LEE, WHERE SHOULD WE DRAW THE NEW LINE ONCE RICHMOND IS **TAKEN?**

SIR, RICHMOND MUST NOT BE GIVEN UP. IT **SHALL** NOT BE GIVEN UP.

UNDER LEE THE CONFEDERATE ARMY STARTED TO HAVE MORE SUCCESS. MCCLELLAN HAD A LARGER FORCE BUT STILL LEE'S SOLDIERS TOOK THEM ON. IN FIVE BATTLES FOUGHT OVER SEVEN DAYS, THE CONFEDERATES DROVE THE UNION ARMY ALL THE WAY BACK TO THE JAMES RIVER.

THE CONFEDERATES WON AT GAINES MILL...

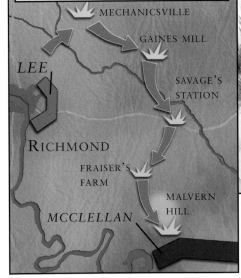

MECHANICSVILLE

GAINES MILL

LEE

SAVAGE'S STATION

RICHMOND

FRAISER'S FARM

MALVERN HILL

MCCLELLAN

...AND WERE BEATEN AT MALVERN HILL.

EVEN THOUGH THE UNION SOLDIERS WON **FOUR** OUT OF THE **FIVE** BATTLES, MCCLELLAN **STILL** RETREATED. HE THOUGHT HE WAS SAVING A **DOOMED** ARMY. THE TIME HAD COME FOR MCCLELLAN TO BE REPLACED.

THE WAR WAS NOT GOING WELL. IN SEPTEMBER 1862, UNION TROOPS SUFFERED A SECOND DEFEAT AT MANASSAS.

GET ME MCCLELLAN.

BUT THE PRESIDENT DID NOT CARE.

WE'RE RIGHT BACK WHERE WE STARTED EXACTLY A YEAR AGO.

THE REAPPOINTMENT OF GENERAL MCCLELLAN WAS NOT POPULAR WITH LINCOLN'S ADVISERS.

HE CAN'T FIGHT, BUT HE IS GOOD AT MAKING OTHERS READY TO FIGHT.

A FEW WEEKS LATER, LEE AND HIS FORCES HEADED NORTH FOR THE FIRST TIME. HE DIVIDED HIS 50,000 MEN INTO FIVE SMALLER ARMIES SO THEY COULD ATTACK THE TOWN OF HARRISBURG, PENNSYLVANIA. EACH OF THE FIVE COMMANDERS WAS GIVEN A WRITTEN PLAN.

MCCLELLAN'S ARMY WAS SENT TO STAND BETWEEN LEE AND **WASHINGTON**. WHILE ADVANCING, THEY CAME UPON A PIECE OF PAPER WRAPPED AROUND THREE CIGARS.

IT'S LEE'S PLANS! WE MUST GET THIS TO HIGH COMMAND!

LEE HEARD ABOUT HIS **MISSING ORDERS**. HE HAD TO MAKE A DECISION.

WE WILL STAND AND **FIGHT**...

LEE'S FORCE OF **20,000** TOOK BATTLE POSITIONS OUTSIDE THE SMALL TOWN OF SHARPSBURG, MARYLAND.

MCCLELLAN'S 75,000 SOLDIERS BEGAN SHOOTING AT THEM ACROSS A WIDE FRONT.

SEPTEMBER 17, 1862, WAS TO BECOME THE BLOODIEST DAY ON AMERICAN SOIL.

OVER **8,000 MEN** LOST THEIR LIVES IN SOME OF THE MOST FEROCIOUS FIGHTING EVER SEEN. IMPORTANT BATTLES WERE FOUGHT AT **THE CORNFIELD, THE SUNKEN ROAD**, AND, FINALLY, AT **ANTIETAM CREEK**.

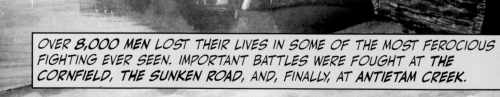

TECHNICALLY, NEITHER SIDE WON THE BATTLE AT ANTIETAM, BUT IT WAS **SEEN** IN THE NORTH AS A UNION VICTORY. ON THE STRENGTH OF THIS PUBLIC FEELING, LINCOLN DECIDED TO MAKE AN IMPORTANT STATEMENT.

"...ALL PERSONS HELD AS **SLAVES** WITHIN ANY STATE, OR DESIGNATED PART OF A STATE, THE PEOPLE WHEREOF SHALL THEN BE IN **REBELLION** AGAINST THE UNITED STATES, SHALL BE THEN, **THENCEFORWARD, AND FOREVER FREE...**"

THE EMANCIPATION PROCLAMATION OF SEPTEMBER 1862 MADE THE CONFLICT A WAR TO FREE THE SLAVES AS WELL AS TO SAVE THE UNION.

MEANWHILE, MCCLELLAN CLAIMED HIS MEN WERE **TIRED** AND HE REFUSED TO GO FORWARD. IN NOVEMBER, LINCOLN REMOVED HIM FROM COMMAND.

"GET ME BURNSIDE."

AMBROSE BURNSIDE HAD PERFORMED WELL AT **ANTIETAM**. LINCOLN HOPED HE MIGHT CHASE THE CONFEDERATE ARMY MORE SERIOUSLY THAN MCCLELLAN.

BURNSIDE PLANNED TO MARCH ON FREDERICKSBURG, VIRGINIA, AND PRETEND TO ATTACK LEE FROM THE FRONT. MEANWHILE, MOST OF HIS ARMY WOULD MARCH SOUTH, CROSS THE RAPPAHANNOCK RIVER AND SURPRISE THE ENEMY FROM THE BACK. BUT THE **PONTOON BRIDGES** HE NEEDED TO CROSS THE RIVER WERE **DELAYED**, GIVING LEE TIME TO **PREPARE**.

ON DECEMBER 13, 1862, BURNSIDE DECIDED TO ATTACK **ANYWAY**.

THE FIRST BRIGADE MARCHED UP THE MARYE'S HEIGHTS TOWARD LEE'S FORCES...

...ONLY TO BE CUT DOWN IN A **HAIL** OF LEAD AND CANNON FIRE.

WAVE AFTER WAVE FOLLOWED, EACH WITH THE SAME RESULT.

THE **COURAGE** OF THE UNION MEN KNEW NO BOUNDS, AS OVER 12,000 OF THEM MARCHED UP THE HILL **KNOWING** THEY WERE GOING TO DIE.

IT WAS A TERRIBLE UNION DEFEAT. IN THE EVENING, GENERAL LEE CAME TO LOOK AT THE BATTLEFIELD.

OH, NO...

"...IT IS AS WELL THAT WAR IS SO **TERRIBLE** OR WE MIGHT GROW TOO **FOND** OF IT."

THE FREDERICKSBURG DISASTER MADE LINCOLN MISERABLE.

WE'VE LOST 12,000 MEN! WHAT CAN I DO WITH SUCH GENERALS AS WE HAVE?

STANTON, GET ME HOOKER!

COMMAND OF THE EASTERN ARMY WAS PASSED TO **GENERAL JOSEPH HOOKER**, WHO VOWED NOT TO MAKE THE SAME MISTAKES AS BURNSIDE. HE LEFT HALF OF HIS MEN AT FREDERICKSBURG AS A **DIVERSION**, WHILE HE MARCHED THE OTHER HALF THROUGH THE FOREST TO SURPRISE LEE FROM THE BACK. BUT THE WILY SOUTHERN GENERAL SAW WHAT HE WAS UP TO. AGAINST ALL MILITARY LOGIC, LEE DIVIDED HIS SMALLER FORCE INTO TWO. ONE PART STAYED TO DEFEND FREDERICKSBURG, WHILE THE OTHER WENT TO **MEET** HOOKER'S ARMY.

LEE DIVIDED HIS ARMY YET AGAIN, AND SENT JACKSON AND 28,000 MEN THROUGH THE FOREST. THEY MARCHED **AROUND** HOOKER'S LINES TO ATTACK, DRIVING THE UNION MEN BACK TO THEIR BASE AT CHANCELLORSVILLE.

HOOKER, KNOCKED SENSELESS BY A CANNONBALL, DELAYED IN GIVING THE ORDER TO RETREAT.

CHANCELLORSVILLE (MAY 1-4, 1863) COST THE UNION 17,000 MEN.

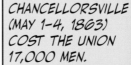

WHAT WILL THE COUNTRY **SAY?**

MEANWHILE, MANY OF THE WOUNDED WERE TRAPPED IN THE THICK FOREST AND BURNED ALIVE IN THE FIRES THAT STARTED.

THE CONFEDERATES LOST "STONEWALL" JACKSON, TO FRIENDLY FIRE.

IN THE WEST, UNION TROOPS WERE BUSY POUNDING VICKSBURG **FROM THE LAND.**

THEY HAD **FAILED** TO BREAK THE TOWN, THAT WAS HIGH ABOVE THE RIVER, FROM THE WATER SO GENERAL GRANT MARCHED HIS ARMY 180 MILES IN 21 DAYS TO GET AROUND AND ATTACK IT **FROM BEHIND.**

GRANT PREPARED FOR A SIEGE.

GENERAL SHERMAN, THESE **MISSISSIPPIANS** JUST DON'T KNOW **WHEN TO SURRENDER.**

MEANWHILE, JEFFERSON DAVIS MET WITH LEE.

I WANT GRANT **TAKEN CARE OF.** VICKSBURG MUST BE HELPED.

SIR, I HAVE A **BETTER** IDEA. WHAT IF GRANT HAD TO LEAVE VICKSBURG TO **DEFEND WASHINGTON?**

SO LEE INVADED **PENNSYLVANIA.**

HOOKER'S ARMY SHADOWS LEE'S, BUT HOOKER WANTS TO DO NOTHING! I THINK IT'S TIME FOR A FRESH HORSE.

TWO SOLDIERS WERE SENT TO FIND **GENERAL GEORGE MEADE** IN THE FIELD.

WAKE UP, SIR. I HAVE IMPORTANT NEWS!

OH, DON'T SAY! HOOKER'S FIRED ME, HASN'T HE?

NO, SIR, IT'S MUCH WORSE THAN THAT. YOU'RE THE NEW COMMANDER!

MEADE TOOK CONTROL OF THE UNION TROOPS SHADOWING LEE'S FORCES. NO ONE KNEW WHEN THE TWO FORCES WOULD MEET. MEANWHILE, A DIVISION OF CONFEDERATE SOLDIERS WAS LOOKING FOR A HIDDEN UNION STOCKPILE OF SHOES IN A NEARBY TOWN. THIS LED TO THE BATTLE OF **GETTYSBURG,** JULY 1-3, 1863.

THE CONFEDERATES NEARED THE TOWN...

QUICK BOYS, IT'S UNION CAVALRY!

A FIGHT BROKE OUT. REBELS AND UNION MEN MOVED CLOSER TOGETHER. GENERAL LEE ARRIVED TO EXAMINE THE SITUATION AS BOTH SIDES TOOK THEIR POSITIONS.

Culp's Hill

Seminary Ridge

Cemetery Ridge

Peach Orchard

Wheatfield

Little Round Top

Big Round Top

WE WILL FIGHT.

GENERAL MEADE ARRIVED THAT EVENING.

THE NEXT MORNING, MEADE SENT SOME UNION MEN UP TO LITTLE ROUND TOP.

"REBS COMIN' UP THE HILL! IF THEY GET CANNONS UP HERE, IT'S ALL OVER!"

MEN, WAVE YOUR FLAGS! MAKE YOURSELVES LOOK LIKE A DIVISION! I'M GOING FOR HELP.

IT TURNED INTO A RACE TO THE PEAK OF LITTLE ROUND TOP...

...WHICH WAS JUST WON BY THE UNION FORCE OF THE 20TH MAINE.

ZING!

CRACKK!

AAGH!

FIERCE FIGHTING CONTINUED THROUGHOUT THE DAY AT THE PEACH ORCHARD, IN THE WHEATFIELD, AND ON THE ROUND TOPS. LEE TRIED TO FOLD MEADE'S ARMY IN ON ITSELF, BUT AT THE DAY'S END THE UNION WERE STILL HOLDING FIRM.

AT GENERAL MEADE'S HEADQUARTERS...

I HAVE A FEELING THAT LEE WILL ATTACK US IN THE CENTER TOMORROW...

THEN WE WILL DEFEAT HIM.

IN THE CONFEDERATE CAMP...

GENERAL LEE, SIR, IT IS MY OPINION THAT NO 15,000 MEN EVER ASSEMBLED FOR BATTLE CAN **TAKE** THAT POSITION.

GENERAL LONGSTREET, THE ENEMY IS **THERE** AND I **MEAN** TO ATTACK HIM.

AT 1:00 P.M. THERE WAS A MIGHTY ROAR AS 170 CONFEDERATE CANNONS LET LOOSE ON THE UNION POSITIONS.

BABOOM!

UP MEN AND TO YOUR POSTS! DON'T FORGET TODAY THAT YOU ARE FROM OLD VIRGINIA!

THREE HOURS LATER, THE GUNS WERE SILENCED. THE CONFEDERATE INFANTRYMEN BEGAN TO ASSEMBLE. THEY WERE LED BY **BRIGADIER GENERAL PICKETT.**

THEN THE 17,000 MEN CLOSED RANKS AND BEGAN THE MARCH FORWARD.

ON THE UNION FRONTLINE, THEY SAW THE CONFEDERATES ADVANCE...

COLLECT ALL THE LOOSE WEAPONS YOU CAN FIND, CLEAN AND LOAD THEM.

PICKING UP SPEED, THE **CONFEDERATES** LET OUT AN EAR-PIERCING YELL AND **CHARGED AS ONE** AT THE UNION CENTER.

CRACKLE!

ROAAAAAR!

BLAST!

SOON THE ENTIRE UNION LINE WAS ABLAZE WITH GUNFIRE.

GIVE 'EM **COLD STEEL**, BOYS!

PICKETT'S MEN WERE DRIVEN **BACK.** THE CHARGE HAD **FAILED.**

LEE RODE OUT TO MEET THE SURVIVORS.

PICKETT, RALLY YOUR DIVISION TO FIGHT BACK!

GENERAL LEE, I **HAVE** NO DIVISION.

IT WAS THE TURNING POINT. FROM NOW ON, LEE WOULD WAGE A WAR ONLY OF **DEFENSE.**

WASHINGTON, JULY 7, 1863.

GRANT'S CAPTURED VICKSBURG!

GLORIOUS NEWS, NICOLAY! CONTROL OF THE MISSISSIPPI IS NOW IN **OUR** HANDS!

LINCOLN MADE JULY 4, THE DAY THE CONFEDERATES SURRENDERED VICKSBURG, A NATIONAL DAY OF THANKSGIVING.

IT WOULD BE 80 YEARS BEFORE VICKSBURG ITSELF WOULD CELEBRATE THAT DAY.

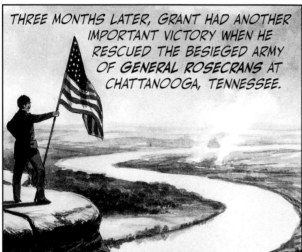

THREE MONTHS LATER, GRANT HAD ANOTHER IMPORTANT VICTORY WHEN HE RESCUED THE BESIEGED ARMY OF **GENERAL ROSECRANS** AT CHATTANOOGA, TENNESSEE.

MEANWHILE, IN WASHINGTON, LINCOLN DECIDED TO GO TO GETTYSBURG, WHERE THE BATTLEFIELD WOULD BE MADE INTO A NATIONAL CEMETERY.

NOVEMBER 19, 1863.

FIRST, A TOUR OF THE BATTLEFIELD.

THEN, AFTER THE GUEST SPEAKER HAD FINISHED...

AND NOW **PRESIDENT LINCOLN** WOULD LIKE TO SAY A FEW WORDS.

"FOUR SCORE AND SEVEN YEARS AGO OUR FATHERS BROUGHT FORTH ON THIS CONTINENT A NEW NATION, CONCEIVED IN LIBERTY AND DEDICATED TO THE PROPOSITION THAT ALL MEN ARE CREATED EQUAL...

...NOW WE ARE ENGAGED IN A GREAT CIVIL WAR, TESTING WHETHER THAT NATION, OR ANY NATION SO CONCEIVED AND SO DEDICATED, CAN LONG ENDURE. WE ARE MET ON A GREAT BATTLEFIELD OF THAT WAR...

...WE HAVE COME TO DEDICATE A PORTION OF THAT FIELD AS A FINAL RESTING PLACE FOR THOSE WHO HERE GAVE THEIR LIVES THAT THAT NATION MIGHT LIVE. IT IS ALTOGETHER FITTING AND PROPER THAT WE SHOULD DO THIS. BUT IN A LARGER SENSE, WE CANNOT DEDICATE, WE CANNOT CONSECRATE, WE CANNOT HALLOW THIS GROUND. THE BRAVE MEN, LIVING AND DEAD WHO STRUGGLED HERE HAVE CONSECRATED IT FAR ABOVE OUR POOR POWER TO ADD OR DETRACT.

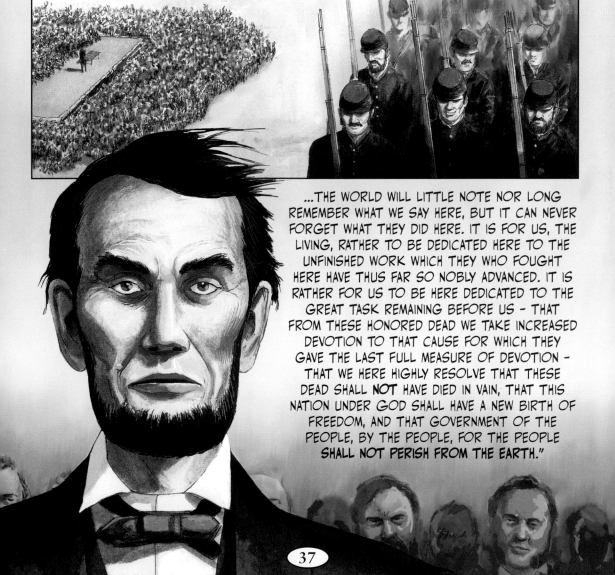

...THE WORLD WILL LITTLE NOTE NOR LONG REMEMBER WHAT WE SAY HERE, BUT IT CAN NEVER FORGET WHAT THEY DID HERE. IT IS FOR US, THE LIVING, RATHER TO BE DEDICATED HERE TO THE UNFINISHED WORK WHICH THEY WHO FOUGHT HERE HAVE THUS FAR SO NOBLY ADVANCED. IT IS RATHER FOR US TO BE HERE DEDICATED TO THE GREAT TASK REMAINING BEFORE US – THAT FROM THESE HONORED DEAD WE TAKE INCREASED DEVOTION TO THAT CAUSE FOR WHICH THEY GAVE THE LAST FULL MEASURE OF DEVOTION – THAT WE HERE HIGHLY RESOLVE THAT THESE DEAD SHALL **NOT** HAVE DIED IN VAIN, THAT THIS NATION UNDER GOD SHALL HAVE A NEW BIRTH OF FREEDOM, AND THAT GOVERNMENT OF THE PEOPLE, BY THE PEOPLE, FOR THE PEOPLE SHALL **NOT PERISH FROM THE EARTH.**"

IN MARCH 1864, A SHORT, DUSTY-LOOKING MAN ARRIVED IN WASHINGTON WITH HIS YOUNG SON.

LATER THAT EVENING, THE MAN MADE HIS WAY TO A PARTY AT LINCOLN'S WHITE HOUSE.

WHY, HERE IS GENERAL GRANT. WELL, THIS IS A GREAT PLEASURE, I ASSURE YOU!

LATER...

I WISH TO EXPRESS MY ENTIRE SATISFACTION WITH WHAT YOU HAVE DONE UP 'TIL NOW. THE PARTICULARS OF YOUR PLANS I NEITHER KNOW NOR SEEK TO KNOW.

GENERAL GRANT WAS GIVEN COMMAND OF THE ENTIRE UNION ARMY, EAST **AND** WEST.

OUR OBJECT IS THE POSSESSION OF LEE'S ARMY...

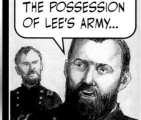

...AND I AM DETERMINED THAT WHEREVER HE GOES, **WE** WILL GO.

LEE WAS DETERMINED TO DRAW OUT THE WAR. HE HOPED LINCOLN WOULD **LOSE** THE COMING ELECTION. HE ALSO HOPED TO MAKE A DEAL WITH THE NEW PRESIDENT.

THE NEXT MONTH, THE 110,000-STRONG ARMY OF THE POTOMAC MARCHED SOUTH TO MEET **LEE'S FORCE** OF 60,000. BEGINNING WITH THE **SECOND BATTLE OF THE WILDERNESS**, IT WAS TO BE SIX BLOODY WEEKS OF FIGHTING. GRANT DESPERATELY ATTEMPTED TO GET HIS ARMY AROUND LEE'S, WHILE LEE **OUTFLANKED** HIM AT EVERY TURN.

AT SPOTSYLVANIA, THE CONFEDERATES WERE CRUSHED AT A PLACE KNOWN AS THE BLOODY ANGLE...

...BUT AT COLD HARBOR THE UNION LOST 7,000 MEN IN **20 MINUTES** WHEN THEY CHARGED THE CONFEDERATE POSITIONS.

WILDERNESS II

SPOTSYLVANIA

GRANT

LEE

COLD HARBOR

RICHMOND

PETERSBURG

THEN GRANT MADE AS IF TO ATTACK RICHMOND, BUT INSTEAD CROSSED THE JAMES RIVER AND MARCHED ON PETERSBURG TO THE SOUTH.

LINCOLN SENT A TELEGRAM.

Lieutenant General Grant

I begin to see it. You will succeed.

A Lincoln

PETERSBURG **ALMOST** FELL BUT UNION DELAY AND THE ARRIVAL OF CONFEDERATE REINFORCEMENTS SAVED THE TOWN. THE TWO SIDES DUG IN FOR A SIEGE.

IN WASHINGTON, LINCOLN'S RE-ELECTION WAS LOOKING UNLIKELY, WITH SO MANY MEN LOST IN GRANT'S CAMPAIGN AND DEADLOCK IN THE EAST.

SEWARD, I AM GOING TO BE BEATEN, AND UNLESS SOME GREAT CHANGE TAKES PLACE, **BADLY** BEATEN.

THE LAST HOPE OF A VICTORY BEFORE VOTING DAY NOW LAY IN THE WEST WITH GENERAL SHERMAN.

THE PREVIOUS MONTH SHERMAN HAD BEEN ORDERED TO MARCH ON ATLANTA. HE ADDRESSED HIS TROOPS BEFORE SETTING OFF.

WAR IS THE REMEDY OUR ENEMIES HAVE CHOSEN...

...AND I SAY LET'S GIVE THEM ALL THEY WANT...

...NOT A WORD OF ARGUMENT, NOT A SIGN OF LET-UP, **NO CAVE IN** UNTIL **WE** ARE WHIPPED – OR **THEY** ARE.

IN SEPTEMBER, THE CITY OF ATLANTA FELL.

MEANWHILE, IN THE CONFEDERATE STRONGHOLD OF THE SHENANDOAH VALLEY, UNION **GENERAL PHILIP SHERIDAN** WAS BUSY RALLYING HIS RETREATING TROOPS.

DON'T CHEER **ME**. FIGHT! WE WILL LICK THEM OUT OF THEIR BOOTS!

THE MEN REFORMED AND WON THE BATTLE. FOR THE FIRST TIME, THE VALLEY NOW BELONGED TO THE UNION.

VOTING DAY ARRIVED. LINCOLN'S DEMOCRAT RIVAL WAS GEORGE B. MCCLELLAN, FORMER UNION GENERAL.

MCCLELLAN WAS RUNNING ON AN ANTI-WAR TICKET, SO THE MEN OF THE ARMY VOTED FOR LINCOLN. HE WAS ELECTED FOR A SECOND TERM.

I GIVE THANKS TO THE ALMIGHTY FOR THIS EVIDENCE OF THE PEOPLE'S RESOLUTION TO STAND BY FREE GOVERNMENT AND THE RIGHTS OF HUMANITY.

MEANWHILE, IN THE SOUTH, SHERMAN WAS WATCHING ATLANTA BURN...

"WE CANNOT CHANGE THE HEARTS OF THESE PEOPLE OF THE SOUTH...

...BUT WE CAN MAKE WAR SO **TERRIBLE**, AND MAKE THEM SO **SICK** OF WAR THAT GENERATIONS WILL PASS AWAY BEFORE THEY AGAIN APPEAL TO IT..."

NOW SHERMAN WANTED TO TAKE HIS ARMY AND TRAVEL 285 MILES THROUGH THE HEART OF THE SOUTH TO REACH THE ATLANTIC OCEAN.

LINCOLN AGREED TO IT, BUT HE WAS WORRIED.

I KNOW THE HOLE HE WENT IN AT, BUT I CAN'T TELL WHAT HOLE HE'LL COME **OUT** OF.

FIVE WEEKS LATER, ABE RECEIVED A TELEGRAM.

"I BEG TO PRESENT TO YOU, AS A CHRISTMAS GIFT, **THE CITY OF SAVANNAH...**"

SHERMAN, WHO WAS ALL FOR "TOTAL WAR," HAD DONE AS PROMISED. HE HAD CUT A SAVAGE PATH 100 MILES WIDE THROUGH THE STATE OF GEORGIA.

LINCOLN WAS DELIGHTED.

GRANT HAS THE BEAR BY THE HIND LEG, WHILE SHERMAN TAKES OFF ITS HIDE!

BUT THAT "HIND LEG" WAS PROVING TROUBLESOME. IN PETERSBURG, THE UNION SIEGE WAS GRINDING ON WITH NO END IN SIGHT.

MARCH 4 1865, INAUGURATION DAY.

WITH MALICE TOWARD **NONE**; WITH CHARITY FOR **ALL**; LET US STRIVE ON TO FINISH THE WORK WE ARE IN; TO BIND UP THE NATION'S WOUNDS; TO CARE FOR HIM WHO SHALL HAVE BORNE THE BATTLE, AND FOR HIS WIDOW, AND HIS ORPHAN, TO DO ALL WHICH MAY ACHIEVE AND CHERISH A JUST AND LASTING PEACE AMONG OURSELVES, AND WITH ALL NATIONS."

"...FONDLY DO WE HOPE, FERVENTLY DO WE PRAY, THAT THIS MIGHTY SCOURGE OF WAR MAY SPEEDILY PASS AWAY. YET, IF GOD WILLS THAT IT CONTINUE UNTIL EVERY DROP OF BLOOD DRAWN BY THE **LASH** SHALL BE PAID BY ANOTHER DRAWN WITH THE **SWORD**, SO STILL IT MUST BE SAID, 'THE JUDGMENTS OF THE LORD ARE TRUE AND RIGHTEOUS ALTOGETHER.'

MEANWHILE, AMONG THE CROWD SOMEONE WAS WATCHING...

...AND WAITING.

AFTER HIS SPEECH...

TAD, I'M A **TIRED** MAN...

...PERHAPS THE **TIREDEST** MAN THAT EVER LIVED!

WITH SHERMAN NOW CUTTING THROUGH THE HEART OF SOUTH CAROLINA, IT SEEMED AS THOUGH THE CONFEDERACY'S DAYS WERE AT LAST NUMBERED. ONLY **GENERAL LEE** STILL HUNG ON, ALTHOUGH HIS GRIP WAS LOOSENING.

JEFFERSON DAVIS DENIED HIM THE MEN AND SUPPLIES HE NEEDED.

THEY DO NOTHING WHILE MY ARMY IS **STARVING.**

THEY **WILL** REGRET IT.

LINCOLN MET WITH HIS COMMANDERS TO DISCUSS THE FINAL CAMPAIGN TO WIN THE WAR.

EARLY ON APRIL 2, ACROSS THE WIDE PETERSBURG FRONT, UNION SOLDIERS BEGAN ADVANCING...

...WHILE LEE'S ARMY SLIPPED AWAY ACROSS THE APPOMATTOX RIVER.

IN RICHMOND, THE ENTIRE CONFEDERATE GOVERNMENT LOADED ITSELF INTO WAGONS AND FLED THE CITY.

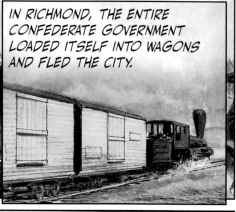

THE FOLLOWING DAY, LINCOLN ARRIVED IN RICHMOND.

IT SEEMS TO ME I HAVE LIVED A HORRIBLE NIGHTMARE FOR FOUR YEARS, AND NOW THAT NIGHTMARE IS OVER.

HE WAS MOBBED IN THE STREETS...

...AND SAT IN PRESIDENT DAVIS'S CHAIR.

OVER THE NEXT FEW DAYS, LEE'S OUTNUMBERED ARMY WAS HOUNDED BY UNION SOLDIERS UNTIL...

IT'S A NOTE FROM LEE. HE'S SURRENDERED!

THE SURRENDER DOCUMENT WAS SIGNED AT A LOCAL HOUSE IN APPOMATTOX, VIRGINIA.

AFTER FOUR BLOODY YEARS THE WAR WAS OVER.

ON APRIL 14, LINCOLN GOT DRESSED FOR A PLEASANT EVENING AT THE THEATER.

THE AUDIENCE CHEERED HIM AS THE BAND PLAYED "HAIL TO THE CHIEF."

BUT SOMEONE WAS COMING...

EVENING, MR. BOOTH!

BANG!

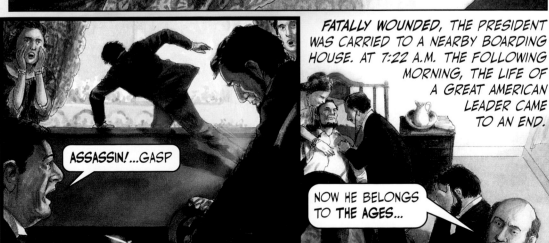

ASSASSIN!...GASP

FATALLY WOUNDED, THE PRESIDENT WAS CARRIED TO A NEARBY BOARDING HOUSE. AT 7:22 A.M. THE FOLLOWING MORNING, THE LIFE OF A GREAT AMERICAN LEADER CAME TO AN END.

NOW HE BELONGS TO **THE AGES...**

THE END

AFTERMATH

*T*he president's assassination was a terrible shock to the war-weary people of America. Abraham Lincoln was only 58 years old when he died. Mary Lincoln never recovered. The recently freed slaves felt as though they had lost their savior.

WHO SHOT LINCOLN?

The actor John Wilkes Booth, a strong believer in slavery, blamed all of America's troubles on the president. He and four accomplices had already failed in one kidnapping attempt on Lincoln. After the assassination, Booth was caught and shot in a barn in Virginia. Many rebel sympathizers were put on trial and the four accomplices were publicly hanged.

The actor John Wilkes Booth fires the fateful shot in this Currier and Ives engraving from 1865.

The Lincoln Memorial in Washington, D.C., is 20 feet (6 meters) high. It is made from blocks of white marble.

THE PRESIDENT REMEMBERED

After lying in state in the White House, the president's body was taken on a 14-day train journey back to his hometown of Springfield. The funeral train stopped in 11 cities, where thousands of mourners lined the streets. Abraham Lincoln was finally laid to rest alongside his son Willie in Oak Ridge Cemetery on May 4, 1865. He would always be remembered for his belief in the ideal of freedom for all people.

FOREVER CHANGED

Apart from ending slavery, Lincoln's government and the Civil War changed America in many ways. Lincoln introduced the first national banking system and issued the first paper currency, known as "greenbacks." With the Homestead Act, he offered free land in the West to those people willing to farm it. He also offered land for building railroads. Before long, it was possible to travel by rail from East to West across the United States.

Before national paper currency was issued, people in the United States traded in goods and metal coins.

Many of these changes were possible because Congress was able to make decisions without consulting the Southern states. The war forced both sides to become war machines that could produce arms efficiently and quickly. It was the beginning of big industry and big business in America. Though the states were reunited after the Civil War, many Southerners still felt a sense of defeat. With 600,000 dead, neither side had much to celebrate. But the war in which three million fought turned into a fight about the meaning of freedom and democracy. It helped shape the United States into the nation it is today.

The might of the North is shown by these large cannons as they prepare to pound Vicksburg, Mississippi in 1863.

GLOSSARY

abolitionist A person who worked to do away with slavery.

accomplice A person who helps others commit a crime.

assassination To murder someone who is well known or important.

avenge To take revenge.

bayonet A long knife that can be attached to the end of a rifle.

bill A written plan for a new law.

buckskins Trousers made from the skin of a deer or sheep.

delegate Someone who represents other people at a meeting.

deport To send someone to another country.

depression Sadness or gloominess.

diversion Something that takes your mind off other things.

doctrine A belief or teaching.

emancipation The freeing of a person or group from slavery or control.

evacuate To move away from an area because it is dangerous.

executive Someone who has a job of great importance.

legislature A group of people who make or change laws.

logic Careful and correct reasoning or thinking.

melancholy Very sad.

militia A fighting unit made up of ordinary citizens.

nomination Being suggested as a candidate, especially for a political office.

opponent Someone who is against you in a fight, contest, or election.

pontoon bridge A temporary, floating bridge.

proclamation A public declaration or announcement.

rebellion When people rise up against their leader or ruler.

siege The surrounding of a place to cut off its supplies.

surveyor Someone who measures land to make a map or plan.

tragedy A very sad event.

tuberculosis A serious disease that affects the lungs.

volunteer Someone who offers to do a job.

Zouaves Soldiers who dressed like the Algerian members of the old French army.

FOR MORE INFORMATION

ORGANIZATIONS

The Abraham Lincoln Museum
Cumberland Gap Parkway (on the grounds of Lincoln Memorial
   University)
Harrogate, TN 37752
(423) 869-6235
Web site: http://www.lmunet.edu/Museum/Main1.htm

The Lincoln Museum
200 E. Berry Street
Fort Wayne, Indiana 46802
(260) 455-3864
Web site: http://www.thelincolnmuseum.org/

FOR FURTHER READING

Blashfield, Jean F. *Abraham Lincoln.* Gettysburg, PA: American
Souvenirs and Gifts, 2000.

Holford, David M. *Lincoln and the Emancipation Proclamation in
American History.* Berkeley Heights, NJ: Enslow Publishers, Inc., 2002.

Judson, Karen. *Abraham Lincoln.* Berkeley Heights, NJ: Enslow
Publishers, Inc., 1998.

Marrin, Albert. *Commander in Chief: Abraham Lincoln and the Civil
War.* New York: Penguin Group, 2003.

Schlesinger Sr., Arthur M., Fred L. Israel, and David J. Frent, eds. *The
Election of 1860 and the Administration of Abraham Lincoln.*
Broomall, PA: Mason Crest Publishers, 2003.

INDEX

A
abolitionists, 6, 18
accomplices, 44
Antietam, 30–31
assassination, 44

B
bayonet, 24
bill, 14–15
Black Hawk, 12
Booth, J. W., 43–44
buckskins, 9
Bull Run, 24

C
Chancellorsville, 32
Confederacy, 20

D
Davis, Jefferson, 3, 21, 33, 42
delegate, 20
Democrats, 6, 13, 20, 40
depression, 7
diversion, 32
doctrine, 16
Douglas, Stephen, 3, 13–17, 20

E
Emancipation Proclamation, 31
executive, 7

F
Farragut, D., 28
Fort Sumter, 21–22
Fredericksburg, 31–32

G
Gettysburg, 33–36
Grant, U. S., 3, 25–28, 33, 36, 38–40

H
Herndon, W., 13, 20
Hooker, J., 32–33

J
Jackson, T. J., 24, 32
Johnston, A., 26
judiciary, 7

L
Lee, R. E., 3, 29–31, 34–35, 38, 42
legislature, 20
logic, 14, 32

M
Manassas, 24, 30
McClellan, G., 3, 25–26, 29–31, 40
melancholy, 12
militia, 21–23, 25

N
New Salem, 11–12
nomination, 18, 20

O
opponent, 16

P
Petersburg, 39–40
pontoon bridges, 31

R
Rappahannock, 31
rebellion, 18, 22, 31
Republicans, 6, 15–16, 18–19

S
Scott, Dred, 15
Sharpsburg, 30
Sherman, W. T., 3, 27, 33, 39–40, 42
Shiloh, 26
siege, 28, 33, 39–40
skirmish, 34
Springfield, 13, 20, 44
surveyor, 12

T
tragedy, 8
tuberculosis, 13

V
Vicksburg, 28, 33, 36
volunteer, 25

W
Whigs, 6, 13

Z
Zouave, 23

Web Sites
Due to the changing nature of Internet links, the Rosen Publishing Group, Inc., has developed an online list of Web sites related to the subject of this book. This site is updated regularly. Please use this link to access the list:

http://www.rosenlinks.com/gnf/lincoln